THE FIRST BOOK OF BARITONE/BASS SOLOS

PART II

compiled by Joan Frey Boytim

G. SCHIRMER, Inc.

DISTRIBUTED BY

HAL•LEONARD®
CORPORATION

7777 W. BLUEMOUND RD. P.O. BOX 13819 MILWAUKEE, WI 53213

PREFACE

The widespread acceptance by teachers and students of "The First Book Series" for Soprano, Mezzo-Soprano/Alto, Tenor, Baritone/Bass has prompted the development of a Part II addition for each voice type. After discussions with numerous voice teachers, the key suggestion expressed many times what that there is a need for "more of the same" type of literature at exactly the same level.

The volumes in Part II follow many of the same concepts which are covered in the Preface of the original volumes, including a comprehensive selection of between 34 and 37 songs from the Baroque through the 20th Century. The selections range from easy to moderate difficulty for both singer and accompanist.

In response to many requests, we have included more sacred songs, and have added to Christmas solos in each volume. The recommendation for more humorous songs for each voice was honored as well.

Even though these books have a heavy concentration of English and American songs, we have also expanded the number of Italian, German, and French offerings. For those using the English singing translations, we have tried to find the translations that are most singable, and in several cases have reworked the texts.

Part II can easily stand alone as a first book for a beginning high school, college, or adult student. Because of the varied contents, Part II can also be successfully used in combination with the first volume of the series for an individual singer. This will give many choices of vocal literature, allowing for individual differences in student personality, maturity, and musical development.

Hal Leonard Publishing (distributor of G. Schirmer) and Richard Walters, supervising editor, have been most generous in allowing the initial objective for this series to be expanded more fully through publishing these companion volumes. We hope this new set of books will provide yet another interesting and exciting new source of repertoire for both the teacher and student

Joan Frey Boytim
September, 1993

About the Compiler...

Since 1968, Joan Frey Boytim has owned and operated a full-time voice studio in Carlisle, Pennsylvania, where she has specialized in developing a serious and comprehensive curriculum and approach to teaching and coaching adolescent and community adult students. Her teaching experience has also included music and choral instruction at the junior and senior high levels, and voice instruction at the college level. She is the author of a widely used bibliography, *Solo Vocal Repertoire for Young Singers* (a publication of NATS), and, as a nationally recognized expert on teaching beginning vocal study, has been featured in many speaking engagements and presentations on the subject.

CONTENTS

L'AMOUR DE MOI

(Love of My Heart)

English version by
Lorraine Noel Finley

15th Century
piano accompaniment
adapted from that of
Julien Tiersot

L'a-mour de moi s'y est en-clo - - se De-dans
Love of my heart is all sur-round - - ed By a

un jo-li jar-di-net, Où croît la rose et le mu-guet Et aus-si
gar-den filled with de-light, Where grow the rose and lil-y white, And they by

fait la pas-se-ro - - se. Ce jar-din est bel et plai-
hol-ly-hocks are bound - - ed. Sweet-ly this gar-den bids me

sant, Il est gar - ni de tou - tes fleurs.
stay, Bright-ly a - dorned by ev - 'ry flow'r.

ben legato

Hé - las! il n'est si dou - ce
Noth-ing more plain - tive ev - er

cho - - se Que de ce doux ros-si - gno-
sound - - ed Than lit-tle night - in-gales in

let Qui chan-te au soir, au ma - ti - net: Quand il est
spring:— All through the night till dawn, they sing; They rest when

las, il se re - po - - se.
tired, their hopes pro - pound - - ed.

Je l'ai re - gar - dée u - ne po - - se: El - le é - tait
There stands my love; I gaze as - tound - - ed; Fresh like a

blan - che com - me lait Et dou - ce comme__ un a - gne -
rose, she lin - gers there, Kind as a lamb,__ and gen - tly

allargando al fine

let, Ver-meil-le et fraî - che com - me ro - - se.
fair; Her life is grace and charm un - bound - - ed.

BRIGHT IS THE RING OF WORDS

Robert Louis Stevenson

Ralph Vaughan Williams

After the sing - er is dead And the mak - er

bur - ied.................... Low as the

sing - er lies In the field of heath - er, Songs of his

fash - ion bring The swains to - geth - er.

And when the west is red With the

sun - set em - - - bers,

la melodia ben marcato.

The lov - er lin - gers and

pp molto più lento.

sings,............... And the maid re-mem - - -bers.

colla voce.

pp molto più lento.

rall.

BLOW, BLOW, THOU WINTER WIND

from *As You Like It*
by William Shakespeare

Thomas Arne

In moderate time

1. Blow, blow,__ thou__ win-ter wind,__ Thou art__ not__ so un-kind,__ thou
2. Freeze, freeze,__ thou__ bit-ter sky,__ Thou dost__ not__ bite so nigh,__ thou

art not so un-kind As man's in-gra - - ti-tude. Thy
dost not bite so nigh As ben - e - fits _____ for-got. Tho'

Printed in the USA by G. Schirmer, Inc.

tooth is not so keen, _____ Be - cause _ thou _ art _ not _ seen, _____ Thy _
thou the wa - ters warp, _____ _____ Thy sting _ is _ not _ so _ sharp, _ Tho'

tooth _ is _ not so _ keen, _____ Be - cause thou art not seen, _ Al -
thou _ the _ wa - ters _ warp, _____ Thy sting is not so sharp _ As

tho' _ thy _ breath be rude, al - tho' _ thy _ breath be rude, _____ al -
friends _ re - mem - ber'd not, as friends _ re - mem - ber'd not, _____ as _

tho' _ thy _ breath _ be _ rude.
friends _ re - mem - ber'd _ not.

BLOW, YE WINDS

sea chantey
arranged by
Celius Dougherty

blow, ye winds, heigh - o. Clear a-way your run-ning gear and

blow, ye winds, heigh - o. They

send you to New Bed - ford, that fa - mous whal-ing port. They

put you on a clip-per ship be - fore you know you're out,— sing - ing,

Blow, ye winds in the morn - ing, blow, ye winds, heigh - o.

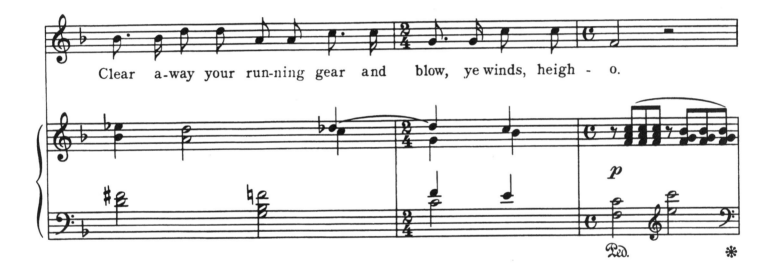

Clear a-way your run-ning gear and blow, ye winds, heigh - o.

It's now we're out to sea, boys, the wind comes on to blow. One

half the watch is sick on deck, the oth-er half be-low, sing-ing,

Blow, ye winds in the morn - ing, blow, ye winds, heigh - o.

Clear a-way your run-ning gear and blow, ye winds, heigh - o.

p

Ped.   *

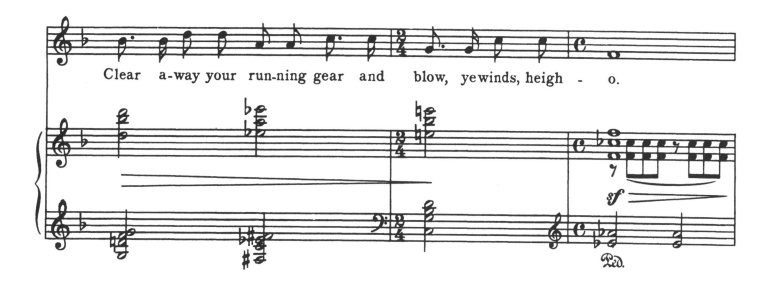

Clear a-way your run-ning gear and blow, ye winds, heigh - o.

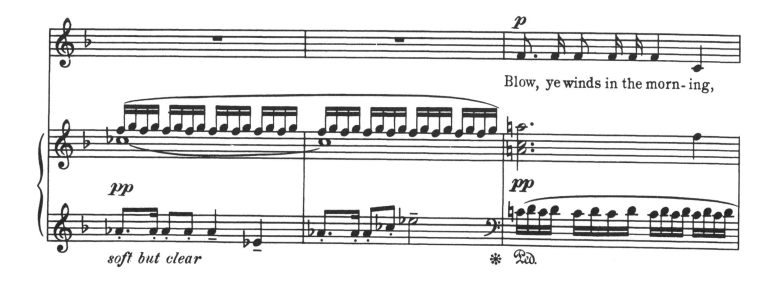

Blow, ye winds in the morn- ing,

soft but clear

in tempo

blow, ye winds, heigh o.

BOIS ÉPAIS

(Sombre Woods)

Jean-Baptise Lully

Bois é - pais re - dou - ble ton
Som - bre woods, ye glades dark and

om - bre, Tu ne sau - rais être as - sez
lone - ly, Where mid - night gloom ___ en - ters

cher   Mon mal - heur - eux ___ a - mour,   Je
love   *In your un - bound - ed night,*   *If*

sens un dès - es - poir   Dont l'hor - reur est ex -
now this bro - ken heart   *Nev - er - more may en -*

trê - me,   Je ne dois plus voir ce que
fold her,   *If no more these eyes may be -*

j'ai - me,   Je ne veux plus souf - frir le
hold her,   *Then ev - er more I hate the*

BUILD THEE MORE STATELY MANSIONS

Oliver Wendell Holmes

Mark Andrews

Build thee more state - ly man-sions, O my soul,— As the swift sea - sons roll,— as the swift sea - sons roll! Build thee more state - ly

man-sions, O my soul,_ more state - ly_ man - sions, O _____ my soul! _

Leave thy low-vault-ed past, leave thy low-vault-ed past, Let each new

tem - ple, no - bler than the last, Shut thee from heav - en with a

dome more vast, _ Till thou at length art free, till thou at length art free,

DEEP RIVER

Spiritual,
arranged by Harry T. Burleigh

Deep _____ riv - er, Lord, I want to cross o - ver in - to camp - ground.

Oh, don't you want _ to go _____ to that gos - pel _____ feast, _____ That

prom - is'd land _____ where all _____ is peace? Oh

deep _____ riv - er, Lord, I want to cross o - ver in - to camp - ground. _____

DOWN HARLEY STREET

Benjamin Musser

Charles Kingsford

he should whis-tle down Har - ley Street; What right has he to keep on whis-tling When

life is so rot-ten that once was sweet? His face shines red as a rus-set ap-ple, His

walk has a swing, there's gold in his hair. Har-ley Street waits for his jol - ly whis-tle, Since

life is a prop-er - ly rot-ten af - fair.

*Melody of final two measures may be whistled.

DU BIST WIE EINE BLUME

(Thou Art Lovely As a Flower)

Heinrich Heine
translation by Charles Fonteyn Manney

Franz Liszt

Printed in the USA by G. Schirmer, Inc.

DU BIST WIE EINE BLUME
(Thou Art Lovely As a Flower)

Heinrich Heine
translation by Charles Fonteyn Manney

Robert Schumann

heart. My hands, in ten-der de-vo-tion, I'd
ein. Mir ist, als ob ich die Hän-de auf's

rest up-on thy hair, Pray-ing that God ev-er
Haupt dir le-gen sollt', be-tend, dass Gott dich er-

keep thee So love-ly, pure and fair.
hal-te so rein und schön und hold.

EIN TON

(What Sound is That?)

text by the composer
translation by J. Ahrem

Peter Cornelius

Un poco agitato.

Mir klingt ein Ton so wun - der -
What sound is that so rich and

bar in Herz und Sin - nen im - mer - dar.
clear? It thrills my heart, it fills my ear;

Ist es der Hauch, der dir ent - schwebt, als ein - mal
Be - lov - ed one, and can it be Thy last fond

als stie - gest lie - bend nie - der du und sän - gest
To soothe my an - guish, calm my grief, And give my

mei - nen Schmerz in Ruh! _____
wound-ed heart re - lief. _____

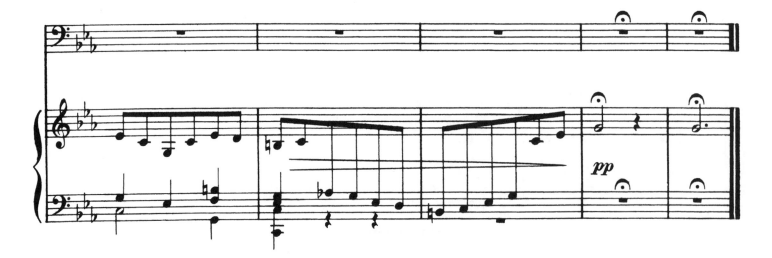

ELDORADO

Edgar Allen Poe

Richard H. Walthew

o'er his heart a sha - - - dow Fell,........

.... as he found No spot of ground That looked like El - do -

- ra - - - do.................

And as his strength Failed him at length, He met a pil - grim

sha - - - dow— "Sha-dow," said he, "Where can it be— This

THE FIRST CONCERT

Sylvia Golden

Mana-Zucca

no - bo - dy home with ___ whom I could stay. A

long - haired man came out to play, He

push hair back

sat at the pian - o and went this way, When all at once he struck the keys, an' I

sneeze **speak** **whistle**

knew it was com-in'! How I did sneeze! Then he played what I thought was a marching song

And be-fore I knew it, I whist-led a - long. Then

ma poked me, an' the ush - er came, And what

speak

ev - er was wrong ___ I got the blame. All was still as he held on one note, And

ff

cough and choke and sputter

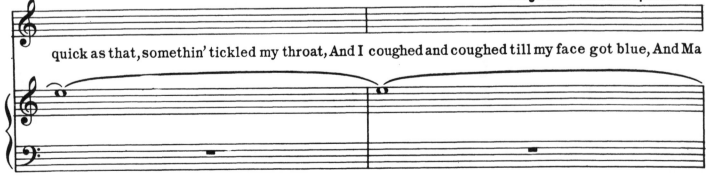

quick as that, somethin' tickled my throat, And I coughed and coughed till my face got blue, And Ma

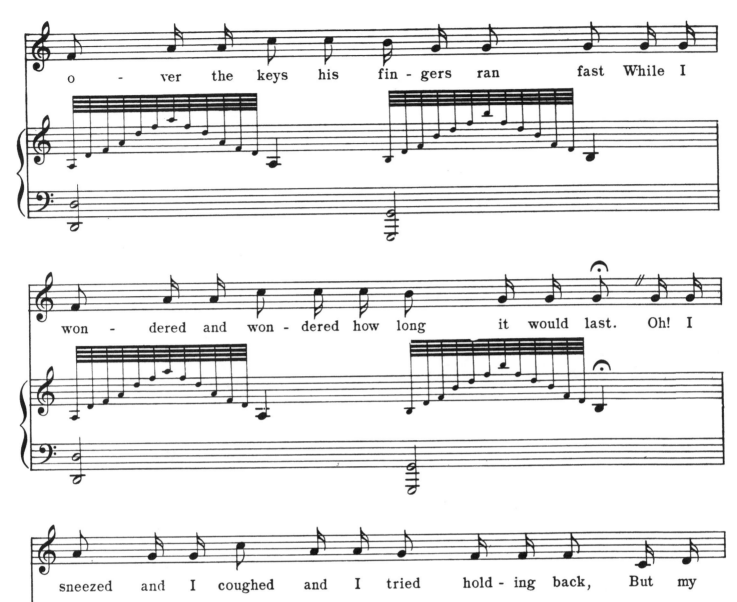

o - ver the keys his fin - gers ran fast While I

won - dered and won - dered how long it would last. Oh! I

sneezed and I coughed and I tried hold - ing back, But my

cough and sputter

breaf got so short,— then an - oth - er at - tack! From a -

head, from be - hind, from the sides, came the shout For the

ush - er to see that my Ma took me out! In a

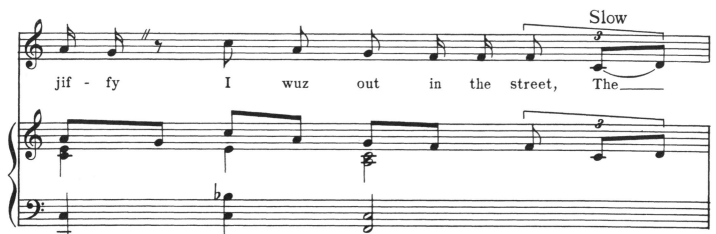

jif - fy I wuz out in the street, The___

first time I felt a real cough was a treat!

GIVE A MAN A HORSE HE CAN RIDE

James Thomson

Geoffrey O'Hara

sea nor shore shall fail!___ Give a man a horse he can ride,___ Give a

man a boat he can sail,___ And his rank and wealth, his strength and health, On

sea nor shore__ shall fail!__ Give a

man a pipe he can smoke,_ Give a man a book he can read__ And his

home is bright with a calm de-light, Tho' the room be poor in - deed.___ Give a

man a pipe he can smoke, Give a man a book he can read,___ And his

home is bright with a calm de-light, Tho' the room be poor in - deed. Give a

man a girl he can love,_____ As I, oh my love, love

GOD IS MY SHEPHERD

paraphrase of Psalm 23

Antonin Dvorák
(from the Biblical Songs)

Andante (quasi recit.)

God is my shep - herd, I want for
Gott ist mein Hir - te, mir wird for nichts

noth - ing. My rest is in the pleas - ant mead - ows, He lead-eth me
man - geln. lunga Er la - gert mich auf grü - ner Wei - de, er lei - tet mich

where qui - et wa - ters flow! My faint - ing soul doth
an stil - len Bä - chen hin! Er labt mein schmachten-

He re - store, and guid - eth me in the ways of peace, to glo - ri -
des Ge - müt und führt mich auf ge - rech - ten We - gen zu sei - nes

Printed in the USA by G. Schirmer, Inc.

fy His name.____
Na - mens Ruhm.____

And though in death's dark val - ley my
Und wall' ich auch im To - des-

steps must wan - der, my spir - it shall__ not fear, for
schat - ten - ta - le, so wall' ich oh - ne Furcht, denn

Thou art by me__ still;
Du be-glei - test__ mich.

Thy__ rod and staff are with me, and
Dein__ Stab ist mei - ne Stüt - ze und

they shall__ com - fort me.
im - mer - dar mein Trost!

THE HEART WORSHIPS

Alice M. Buckton

Gustav Holst

Lyrics: Si - lence in Heav'n—
Si - lence on Earth—
Si - lence with - in Thy

touch to win; Si - lence in

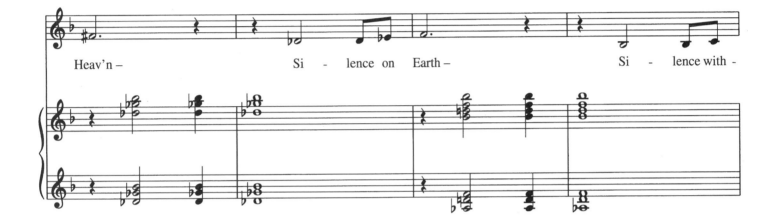

Heav'n – Si - lence on Earth – Si - lence with -

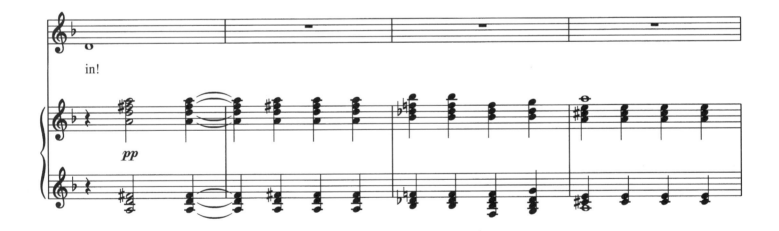

in!

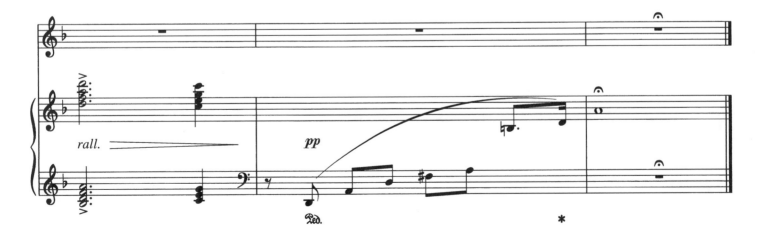

rall. *pp*

IN EINEM KÜHLEN GRUNDE

(Mill of the Valley)

Joseph, Freiherr von Eichendorff

German Folksong

Allegretto.

In ei - nem küh - len Grun - de, da geht ein Müh - len-
On yon - der fleet - ing riv - er There turns a bus - y

rad, _____ mein Lieb - chen ist __ ver - schwun - den, __ das
wheel, _____ My Love has fled; _ ah! sor - row, __ Which

dort ge - woh - net hat, _____ mein Lieb - chen ist __ ver -
time can nev - er heal, _____ My Love, ah! bit - ter

schwun - den __ das dort ge - woh - net hat
sor - row, __ Which time can nev - er heal.

Printed in the USA by G. Schirmer, Inc.

Sie hat mir Treu' ver-spro-chen, gab mir ein'n Ring da-
She gave as true - love to - ken A beau - teous ring of

bei, _____ sie hat die Treu' ge-bro--chen das
gold. _____ The ring is long_ since brok--en, Her

Ring-lein brach ent-zwei, _____ sie hat_ die Treu' ge-
love is dead and cold, _____ Her true_ love, which she

bro--chen, das Ring-lein brach ent-zwei. Hör'
prom--ised, Is past, is dead, and cold. And

ich das Mühl - rad ge - - hen ich weiss nicht, was _ ich
when by chance, in pass - -ing, I view the rest - less

will; _____ ich möcht' am lieb - sten ster - ben,_ da
mill, _____ I wish then all _ was o - -ver, _ My

wär's auf ein - mal still, _____ ich möcht' am lieb - sten
heart were cold _ and still; _____ I wish _ that life _ were

ster - - ben,_ da wär's auf ein - mal still!
o - -ver,_ My heart for - ev - er still!

I WONDER AS I WANDER

Appalachian Carol
adapted and arranged
by John Jacob Niles

Collected by
John Jacob Niles

When Ma-ry birthed Je-sus, 'twas in a cow's stall, With

wise men and farm-ers and shep-herds and all. But high from God's heav-en a

star's light did fall, And the prom-ise of a-ges it then did re-call.

I won-der as I wan-der, out un-der the sky, How

Je-sus the Sav-ior did come for to die For poor on-'ry peo-ple like

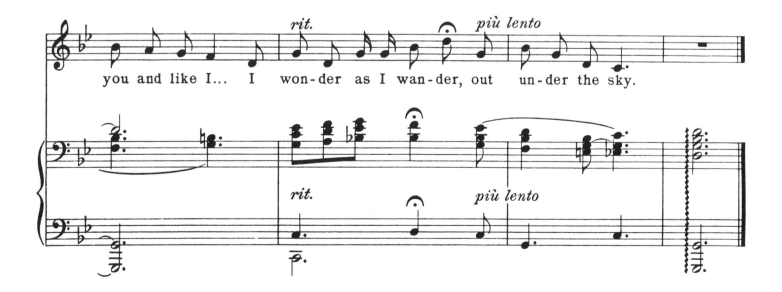

you and like I... I won-der as I wan-der, out un-der the sky.

JESUS, FOUNT OF CONSOLATION

from the *Schmelli Gesangbuch*

translation by Troutbeck

J. S. Bach

might, Death - - less life ____ has brought to ____
more, Fierce - - ly though ____ they rage and ____

light, He ____ is held of ____ Death no ____
roar. Zi - - on right - ly ____ then re - -

long - er, He ____ than Death it - - self ____ is
joi - ces: Sing ____ we all, with ____ hearts ____ and

strong - er. Hal - le - lu - jah! ____ Hal - le - lu - jah!
voi - ces, Hal - le - lu - jah! ____ Hal - le - lu - jah!

DIE KÖNIGE

(The Kings)

text by the composer
revised by Henry Clough-Leighter

Peter Cornelius

OS TORMENTOS DE AMOR

(The Torments of Love)

Brazilian Folksong,
arranged by Edward Kilenyi

LE MIROIR
(The Mirror)

Haraucourt
translation by Lorraine Noel Finley

Gustave Ferrari

Tranquillo e legato

p poco rubato

L'o-deur de vous flot-tait dans l'air si - len - ci - eux: _____
Through-out the qui - et air your fra-grance seemed to rise. _____

p quasi in tempo

J'ai vu la cham-bre vide et la ta - ble lais-
I saw the emp - ty room and the ta - ble va-

rit.

a tempo

sé - e, Le li - vre où pal - pi - tait en - cor vo-tre pen-sé - e, Le mi-
cat - ed, The book where - in your thought still ten-der - ly vi - brat - ed, And the

roir qui lui - sait comme un mor - ceau des ___ cieux.
mir - ror that shone as clear as lam - bent ___ skies.

A - lors, seul, je me suis in - cli -
A - lone there, as I leaned toward these

né vers ces cho - ses, Et j'ai pi - eu - se - ment, de mes deux lè - vres clo -
trea - sures, e - lat - ed, With rev - er - ence I saw the mir-ror all trans - lat- -

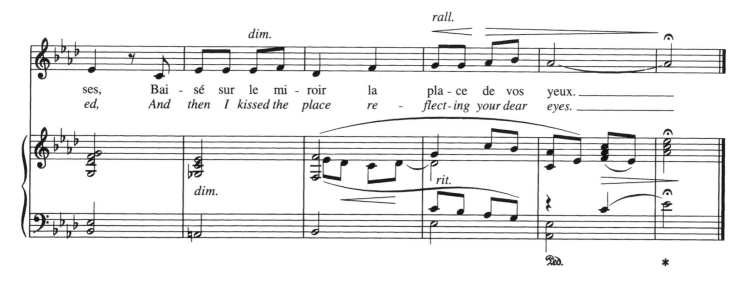

ses, Bai - sé sur le mi - roir la pla - ce de vos yeux. _____
ed, And then I kissed the place re - flect-ing your dear eyes. _____

O'ER THE HILLS

Francis Hopkinson

Allegro spiritoso ($\quarternote$ = 108)

O'er the hills far a-way at the__

birth of the morn, I hear the full____ tone, I

hear the full tone of the sweet sound - ing horn, of the

sweet— sound-ing horn, I

hear the full ___ tone of the sweet sound - ing horn.

The sports - men, with shout-ing, All hail the new day, The

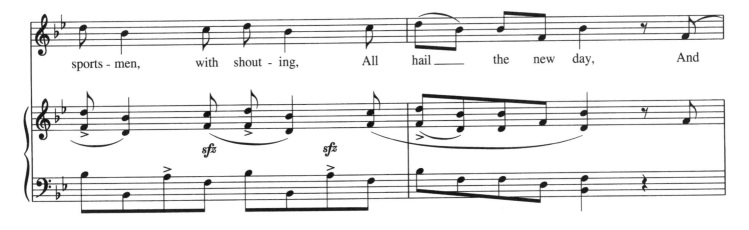

sports - men, with shout - ing, All hail ___ the new day, And

swift run the hounds o'er the hills ___ far a - way. ___

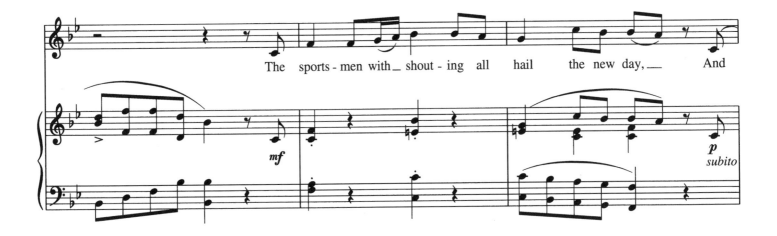

The sports - men with ___ shout - ing all hail the new day, ___ And

swift run ___ the ___ hounds ___ o'er the hills far a - way.

A - cross the deep val - ley their course__ they pur - sue, And

rush thro'__ the __ thick - ets yet sil - ver with dew. And

rush _____ thro' the __ thick - ets yet__ sil - ver with dew. Nor

fenc - es nor ditch - es their speed can de - lay. Still

sounds ___ the sweet horn on the hills far a - way,

Still sounds_ the sweet horn o'er the

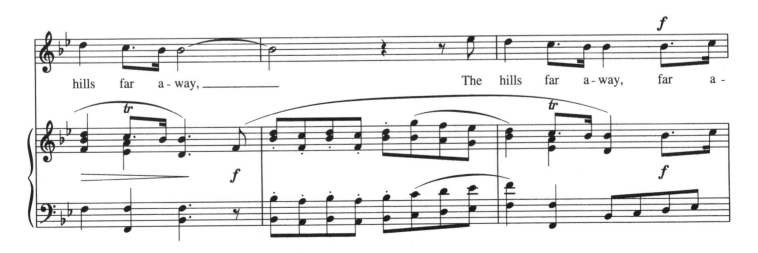

hills far a - way, _____ The hills far a - way, far a -

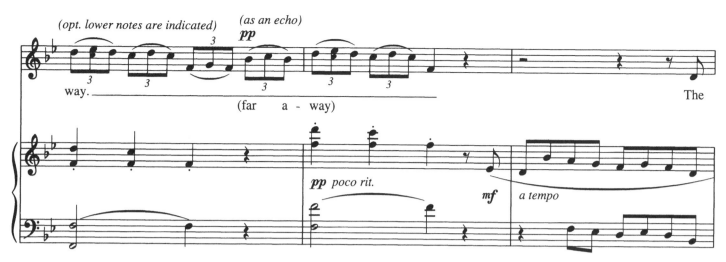

PILGRIM'S SONG

Paul England

Pytor Il'yich Tchaikovsky

My bless-ing fall on this fair world, On mountain, valley, for-est,

o - cean,

più f   *dimin.*

poco cresc.

The clarion winds in ceaseless mo - tion,   And heav'n's blue ban - ner high un -

p

poco cresc.

furl'd_____   And

dimin.

blest the staff__ that hither bore   me,   The alms   that help'd me on my

p cresc

way, The bound - less plain that lies be - fore me, The

glow-ing morn, the eve - - ning grey!

The ver - y path by which I wander Shows glorious,

golden, bath'd in light.

No blade of grass that glistens yon - der

But seems a star from Heaven's height!_____

Oh! might I in my ex - ul - ta - - tion To

all the world this joy im - part!

Would I might clasp the whole cre - a - tion,

Lov - ers or stran - gers, foes or

broth - - ers, Would I might clasp them, the whole cre -

a - tion, with fer - vent rap - ture

to my___ heart!

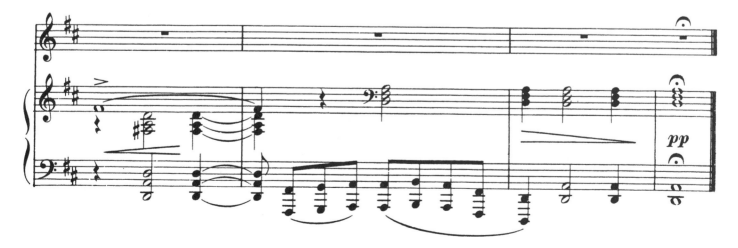

PRETTY AS A PICTURE

from *Sweethearts*

Robert B. Smith

Victor Herbert

poco rit. *poco animato*

all her own, we think, — And as this god - dess goes her way, She

rit. *p*

chuck - les as she hears us say: "She's pret - ty as a pic - ture,

grazioso

Bloom-ing as a rose, Grace in ev - 'ry move-ment, Charm in ev - 'ry

poco rit. *p a tempo*

pose." Ha! ha! O clev - er lit - tle wo-man, We all un - der-stand That

poco rit.

Na - ture can - not make you What you can do by hand. —

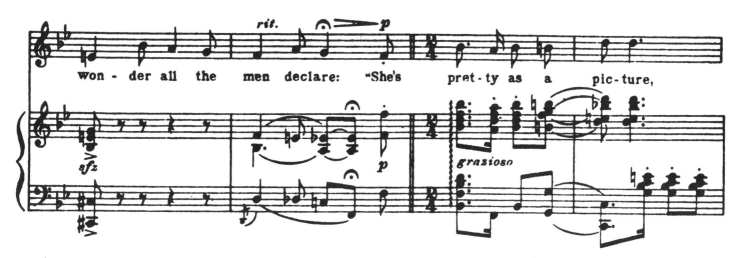

won - der all the men declare: "She's pret - ty as a pic - ture,

Bloom-ing as a rose, Grace in ev - ry move - ment, Charm in ev - ry

pose." Ha! ha! O clev - er lit - tle wo - man, We all un - der - stand That

Na - ture can - not make you What you can do by hand

THE PRETTY CREATURE

Stephen Storace,
arranged by H. Lane Wilson

Allegro vivace

Oh! the pret-ty, pret-ty crea-ture!_____ When I next __ do __

meet her, No __ more like a clown will I face her frown, But

gal - lant - ly will I treat her,_____ But gal - lant - ly

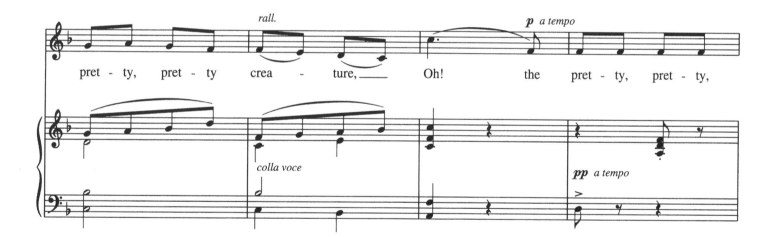

will I treat her._____ Oh! the pret - ty, pret - ty, pret - ty,

pp parlando

f

pp

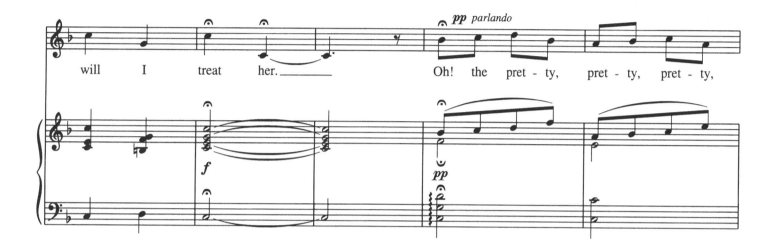

pret - ty, pret - ty crea - ture,_____ Oh! the pret - ty, pret - ty,

rall.

p a tempo

colla voce

pp a tempo

pret - ty, pret - ty crea - ture._____

ff

sf

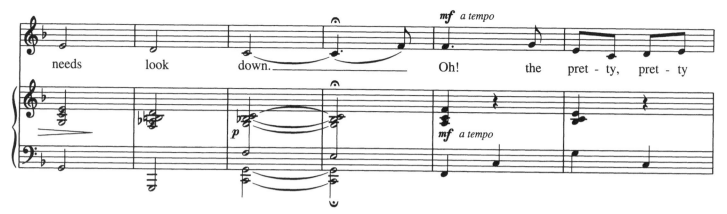

needs look down._____ Oh! the pret - ty, pret - ty

crea - ture,_____ When I next __ do __ meet her, No __

more like a clown will I face her frown, But gal - lant - ly will I

treat her;_____ But gal - lant - ly will I treat her._____

Oh! the pret - ty, pret - ty, pret - ty, pret - ty, pret - ty crea - ture,__ Oh! the

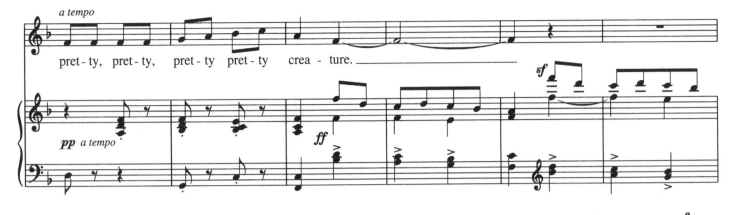

pret - ty, pret - ty, pret - ty pret - ty crea - ture.

Des -

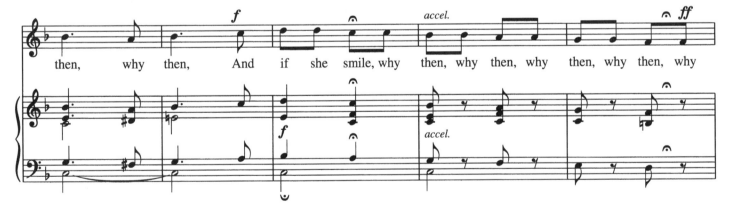

pair gives cour - age oft to men, And if she smile, why

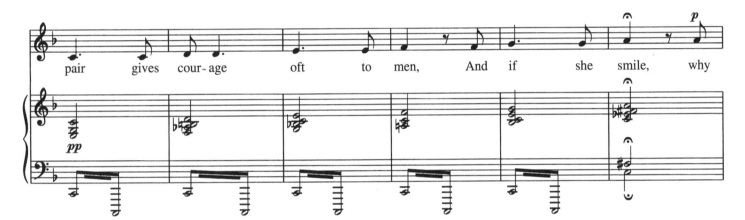

then, why then, And if she smile, why then, why then, why then, why then, why

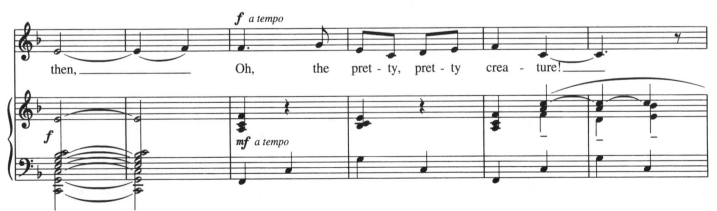

then, _____ Oh, the pret - ty, pret - ty crea - ture! _____

When I next — do — meet her, No — more like a clown will I

face her frown, But gal - lant - ly will I treat her, — But

gal - lant - ly will I treat her. — Oh! the pret - ty,

pret - ty, pret - ty, pret - ty, pret - ty crea - ture, — Oh! — the pret - ty, pret - ty,

pret - ty, pret - ty crea - ture.

THE ROADSIDE FIRE

Robert Louis Stevenson

Ralph Vaughan Williams

I .... will make a pa - lace fit for you and me, Of

green days in fo - rests, and blue days at sea.

I .... will make my

kitch-en, and you shall keep your room, Where white flows the

ri - ver and bright blows the broom; And you .... shall wash your

lin - en, and keep your bo - dy white In rain - fall at

morn - - ing and dew - fall at night.

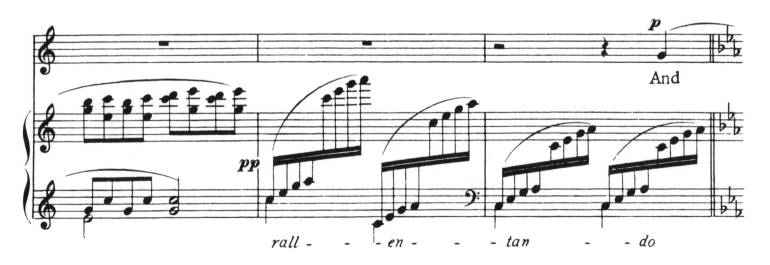

rall - - en - tan - - do

And

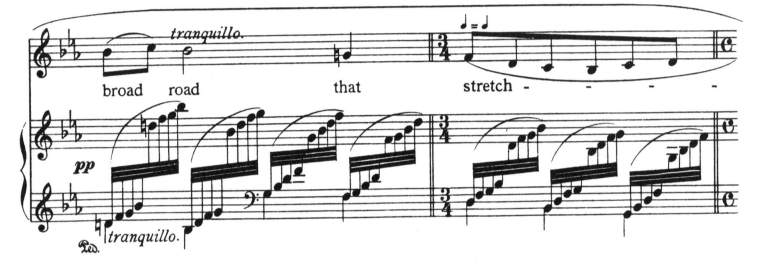

ROLLING DOWN TO RIO

Rudyard Kipling

Edward German

Yes, week-ly from South-

amp-ton, Great ___ steam-ers white and gold, ___ Go ___ roll-ing down to

Ri - o, (Roll ___ down, roll down to Ri - o!) And I'd like to roll to

Ri - o some - day be - fore I'm old! to roll, ___

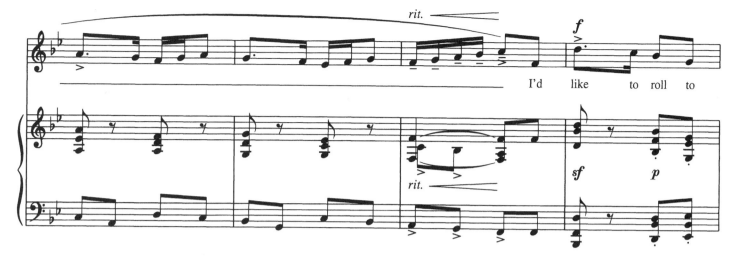

I'd like to roll to

Ri - o some - day be - fore I'm old! _____

I've

nev - er seen a jag - uar nor yet an ar - ma - dill - o

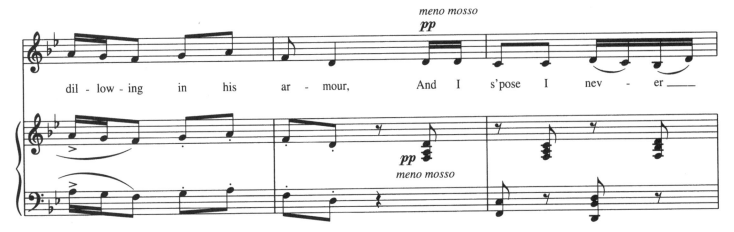

dil - low - ing in his ar - mour, And I s'pose I nev - er ____

will, Ah. _____ Un -

less I go to Ri - o, These ___ won - ders to be - hold, ___ Go ___

roll - ing down to Ri - o Roll ___ real - ly down to Ri - o! Oh, I'd

love to roll to Ri — o some – day be-fore I'm old! to

roll, _____ I'd

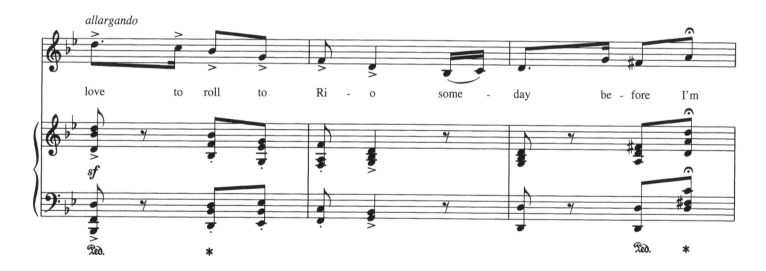

love to roll to Ri — o some – day be-fore I'm

old. _____

THE SLIGHTED SWAIN

17th century English,
arranged by H. Lane Wilson

Tempo di Minuetto

Chlo - e proves false,_____ but still she is charm - ing;

Na - ture, like beau - ty,___ her___ tem - per___ has___ made

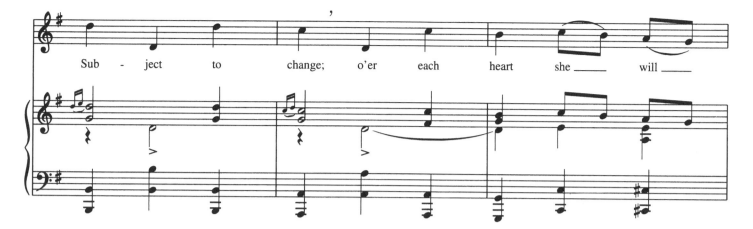

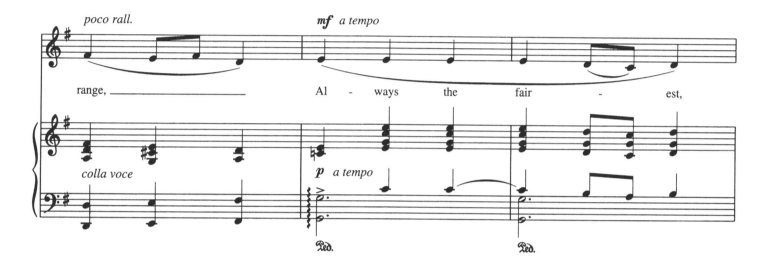

Ban - ish my sen - ses, but let her not slight me,

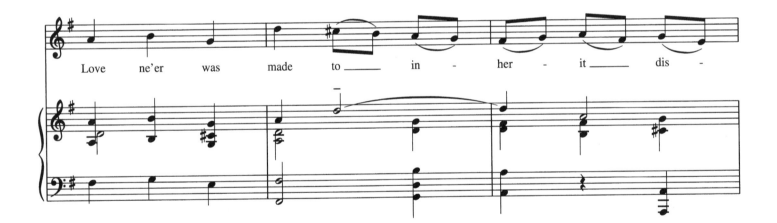

Love ne'er was made to in - her - it dis -

dain; Love is a bub - ble that gives man - kind

trou - ble, Ev - er al - lur - ing, sel - dom en -

dur - ing, Chlo - e who flouts me I sigh for in

vain, Chlo - e who flouts me I sigh for in

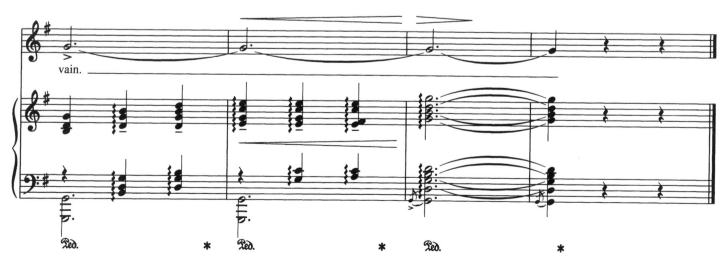

vain.

THE SONG OF MOMUS TO MARS

John Dryden
from "Secular Masque"

William Boyce

Thy Sword with-in the Scab - bard keep, and

let Man - kind _ a - gree;   let Man - kind a - gree; ___   let Man - kind a - gree;

Bet - ter the World were fast a - sleep than kept a - wake by Thee,   than

Printed in the USA by G. Schirmer, Inc.

kept a - wake by Thee; bet - ter the World were fast a - sleep than

kept a - wake by Thee, bet - ter fast a - sleep than

kept a - wake by Thee.

Thy The

Fools are on-ly thin-ner, with all our ___ Cost and Care, But

nei - ther Side a ___ Win - ner, For things are as they ___ were,

cresc. things are as they ___ were, things are ___ as they were The *f*

Fools are ___ on - ly ___ thin - ner with all our ___ Cost and ___ Care, ___ But

nei - ther ___ Side a Win - ner, For things ___ are as they were,

things are as they were, things are as they were;

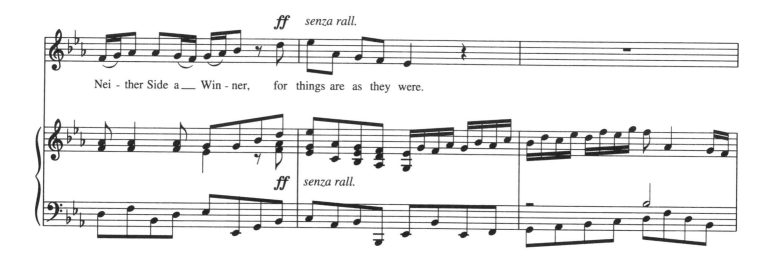

Nei - ther Side a ___ Win - ner, for things are as they were.

The

SEA FEVER

John Masefield

Mark Andrews

wheel's kick, and the wind's song and the white sail's shak-ing, A gray mist on the

sea's face and a gray_____ dawn break-ing.

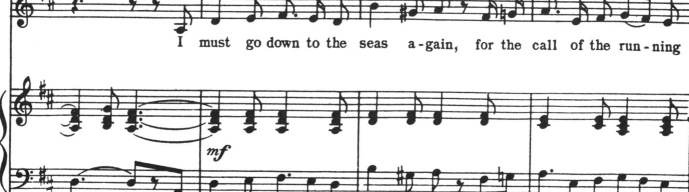

I must go down to the seas a-gain, for the call of the run-ning

tide___ Is a wild call and a clear call, that may not be de - nied;___ And

all I ask is a wind-y day with the white clouds fly-ing, The flung spray and the

blown spume and the sea - - gulls cry-ing. I

poco rit.

must go down to the seas a-gain, to the va-grant gyp-sy

life,___ To the gull's way and the whale's way where the wind's like a whet-ted

knife;___ And all I ask is a mer-ry yarn from a laugh-ing fel-low-

ro-ver, And a qui - et sleep and a sweet dream when the long

Tempo I°

___ trick's o - ver.___ I must go down to the

seas a-gain to the lone-ly sea___ and the sky!___

DIE WETTERFAHNE
(The Weathervane)

Wilhelm Müller
English translation by Theodore Baker

Franz Schubert

Molto vivace.

Now with the vane the wind is toy-ing, That on my sweetheart's
Der Wind spielt mit der Wet-ter-fah-ne auf mei-nes schö-nen

house-top veers!
Lieb-chens Haus.
It seems to me as if 'twere joy-ing In mock-'ry
Da dacht' ich schon in meinem Wahne: sie pfiff den

at my sighs and tears. Had I but notic'd it ere I en-ter'd, The
ar-men Flücht-ling aus. Er hätt' es e-her be-mer-ken sol-len des

fic - kle sym - bol mount - ed there, Ne'er had my fool - ish hopes been cen-tred On
Hau - ses auf - ge - steck - tes Schild, so hätt' er nim - mer su - chen wol-len im

cresc.

dol.

one in - con - stant, tho' so fair.
Haus ein treu - es Frau - en-bild.

With-
Der

f *p* *pp*

in the wind with hearts is play-ing As with the vane, tho' none can see;
Wind spielt drin - nen mit dem Her - zen wie auf dem Dach, nur nicht so laut.

pp

What care they, tho' my heart be dy - ing? Their child a wealth - y
Was fra - gen sie nach mei - nen Schmerzen, ihr Kind ist ei - ne

cresc. *mf* *cresc.*

TOGLIETEMI LA VITA ANCOR
(Take Away My Life)

Take away my life, cruel heavens,
If you wish to steal my heart.
Deny me the light of day, ruthless stars,
If you are happy with my sorrow.

Alessandro Scarlatti

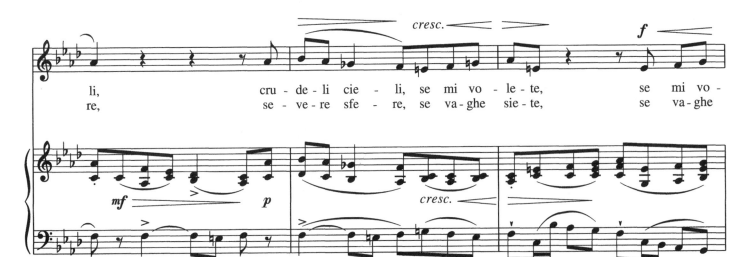

Printed in the USA by G. Schirmer, Inc.

VERRATHENE LIEBE

(Love's Secret Lost)

Adelbert von Chamisso
translation by Frederic Field Bullard

Robert Schumann

oar told the boat-man in glee. And_ he, the boat-man, he sang it To a
Ru - der dem Schif - fer ge - sagt. *Da_ sang der - sel - bi - ge Fi - scher es*

lass with gold - en curls; And_ now in the high-ways and by - ways 'Tis_
sei - ner Lieb - sten vor. *Nun_ sin - gen's auf Stra - ssen und Märk - ten die_*

sung by the boys and the girls!
Kna - ben und Mäd - chen im Chor.

translated into German from
the original English text,
from *Two Gentleman from Verona*
by William Shakespeare

WAS IST SYLVIA?

(Who Is Sylvia?)

Franz Schubert

un - ter - than, _ dass ihr al - les
she might be, _ That a - dor - ed

un - ter - than.
she might be.

Ist sie schön, und gut da -
Is she kind _ as she is

zu? _ Reiz labt wie mil - de Kind - heit;
fair? _ For beau - ty lives with kind - ness:

Ih - rem Aug' _ eilt A - - mor zu, _ dort
To her eyes _ love doth re - pair _ To

heilt er sei - ne Blind - heit, und ver -
help him of his blind - ness; And, be - ing

weilt _ in süs - ser _ Ruh', _ und ver -
help'd, in - hab - its _ there, And, be - ing

weilt in süs — ser _ Ruh'.
help'd, in - hab - its_ there.

Da - rum Syl - via,
Then to Syl - via

tön, o Sang, — der hol - den Syl - via Eh - ren
let us sing, — That Syl - via is ex - cel - ling,

je - - den Reiz ___ be - siegt sie
She ex - cels ___ each mor - - tal

lang, ___ den Er - de kann ge - wäh - ren,
thing ___ Up - on the dull earth dwell - ing;

Krän - - ze ihr und Sai - - ten - klang,
To her gar - lands let us ___ bring,

Krän - ze ihr und Sai - ten - klang.
To her gar - lands let us ___ bring.